For You

Andreas Seidl

Handover of Power

European Version

Volume 11: Free Market Economy

Imprint

Bibliographic information of the German National Library: The German National Library lists this publication in the German National Bibliography; detailed bibliographic data are available on the Internet at http://dnb.dnb.de.

© 2022 Dipl. Pol. Theodor Andreas Seidl

Cover: Christiane Ebrecht
Translation: DeepL, Cologne
Production and publishing: BoD – Books on Demand, Norderstedt

ISBN: 978-3-7568-0259-3

Acknowledgements

My thanks go to my family and friends who have made me who I am today. Special thanks to all those who supported me in writing this book. I would like to thank all my classmates, teachers, fellow students, lecturers, demonstrators, activists, colleagues, companies and countries with whom I have had the privilege of sharing the experiences from which all the ideas in this book have emerged. I would like to thank the staff of Books on Demand for their kind helpfulness. I thank the citizens of Seligenstadt for the harmony and solidarity in which I was able to write.

Foreword

This policy concept contains a variety of proposals for possible political reforms. It can be peacefully and democratically adapted to any current political system of any state in the world, but also to political systems in families, clubs, associations or companies. Wherever humans make or submit to rules that manage living together, the following proposals can be helpful. Readers who find the proposals so helpful that they would like to implement them together with like-minded people can contact the author. The contact form on the last page can be used for this purpose.

Faults and defects

I ask for your understanding that this volume was not professionally proofread. I could only afford professional proofreading for the summary. Spelling errors and unfortunate phrasing may therefore occur. As soon as this volume has sold enough to pay for a professional proofreading, it will be done. After that, a new edition will be published.

English version

Please understand that this volume has been translated automatically. I could only afford a professional translation for the summary. Poor wording and spelling errors may therefore occur. In case of doubt, the German version shall prevail. As soon as this volume has sold enough to pay for a professional translation, it will be done. After that, a new edition will be published. It was more important to me that no one in the world should have an information advantage than individual translation errors in the complete work.

References

If something has been quoted directly, it is set in italics. If the headings contain footnotes, the sources for direct and indirect quotations apply in the chapter for which the heading stands. Otherwise, quotations or source references are directly at the word or at the end of the sentence or paragraph. This book contains parts of text based on the Federal Constitution of the Swiss Confederation of 18 April 1999 (as of 12 February 2017), abbreviated to BV[1] and the Constitution of the Canton of Bern of 6 June 1993 (as of 11 March 2015), abbreviated to KV[2] .

If the constitutional paragraph, or individual paragraphs thereof, are based in whole or in part on extracts from the BV or KV, this is indicated in a footnote. The references to the corresponding footnotes for constitutional paragraphs are usually found after the heading of the affected chapter and sometimes in the body of the text. Articles used in the Swiss constitutions are listed in the footnote with a number after the title of the constitutional paragraph. Example: §123 Sample title: BV Art.123, KV Art.123.

All internet sources are fully cited in the footnotes. They were last accessed on 30.09.2021. All literature sources are also listed in full in the footnotes.

All references to tasks undertaken by other ministries and described in more detail there are given in footnotes. Example: Model Ministry - 1.2.3 Model Chapter.

All footnotes are to be viewed in comparison to the respective source, so-called indirect quotations. Direct quotations are set in italics, but hardly ever occur. The source reference is intended to enable further investigation and to take copyright

---

1 This is not an official publication. Only the publication by the Swiss Federal Chancellery is authoritative. https://www.fedlex.admin.ch/eli/cc/1999/404/de On 14.12.2021

2 This is not an official publication. The Bernese Official Collection of Laws is authoritative. https://www.belex.sites.be.ch/frontend/versions/2420?locale=de#ART71 On 16.12.2021

into account.

All keywords used, based on the names of the responsible units, departments and ministries of Germany, are listed at the end of this volume in the chapter on the conversion of ministries.

Table of contents

1 Goals of the Ministry for Free Market Economy

The Free Market Economy represents a life of freedom and wealth in the four economic forms. The aim of the Free Market Economy is to give companies as much economic freedom as possible. Economic freedom is limited only to prevent damage to other economic forms, consumers, bystanders and the environment. Global trade in goods, money and labour in fair and free competition is the goal of this market economy. The goal is considered achieved when sufficient competition between competitors ensures the best possible price-performance ratio.

2 Departments

The departments are divided into sub-departments and enumerations are usually considered as their individual units. Many tasks of some departments are completely taken over by other ministries as a service.

2.1 Central Department

Part of the Central Department is the Reception Office with the Courier and Mail Room, which directs all concerns, broadcasts and visitors to the appropriate place in the ministry.

2.1.1 Staff

The Human Resources Department is responsible for staff development and planning. For this purpose, it takes care of the recruitment of junior staff, intern and trainee programmes as well as the selection procedures for employees and special selection procedures for applicants with disabilities. For politicians and employees, the department prepares a job plan. In all its tasks, it works in voting with the personnel board.[1]

All other personnel matters are transferred to the relevant ministries. The Ministry of Education is responsible for the training and further education of employees for the

---

1 Ministry of State Organisation - 2.1.1.1 Personnel board

state service.[2] The Ministry of Labour takes over the service law.[3] This includes the labour and collective bargaining law for employees in the state service, remuneration, personnel administration of all careers and employees, flexitime, holiday and sickness records, working time with or without flexitime in part-time or full-time at the place of work or in home work. The Ministry of Infrastructure provides housing assistance for all state employees.[4] The Ministry of Finance's Pay Office takes care of employees' salary, expenses, travel and relocation costs.[5]

The Ministry of Education provides childcare for all employees in the state service.[6]

The Ministry of Health is responsible for the occupational health service.[7] It ensures occupational health management, deals with the treatment, education and prevention of occupational accidents, controls and provides occupational health and safety through the health auditors of the Company Auditing Agency.[8]

2.1.2 Organisation

The ministries of media, security, justice, finance, labour, state organisation provide audit services for quality management in the ministry, evaluation of work performance, revenues and expenditures, as well as corruption prevention, sabotage protection and, if necessary, disciplinary matters.[9]

The language service for translating talks or texts is provided by the Ministry of Education.[10] The Ministry of Finance organises the annual budget vote and ensures proper accounting in each

---

2Ministry of Education - 2.1.1.1 Education and training for the state service
3Ministry of Labour - 4 State enterprises, 13 Labour Directory
4Ministry of Infrastructure - 2.1.1.1 Housing assistance for state service employees
5Ministry of Finance - 2.1.1.1 Staff remuneration
6Ministry of Education - 2.1.1.2 Childcare for state service employees
7Ministry of Health - 2.1.1.1 Occupational Health Service
8Ministry of Labour - 20.7.2 Health auditor
9Ministries of Media, Security, Justice, Finance, State Organisation - 2.1.2.1 Audit services
10Ministry of Education - 2.1.3 Language Service

ministry.[11] It regulates budget procedures, budget law, staff budgets, departmental budgets, costs and cash management, and assists ministries in budget planning for the budget vote. The Ministry of Labour regulates public procurement law and ensures corruption-free state orders and procurement.[12]

The Ministry of Digital Affairs supports the provision of Information Technology (IT).[13] In voting with the Procurement Office of the Ministry of Labour, it takes care of the procurement, provision, maintenance and service of technical devices and software. Much of this is produced in-house to ensure data protection in information and communication technology. Information technology and digitalisation officers audit and advise the ministries. Digital appointment calendar and documentation services are provided as well as a digital policy archive including a library.

2.2 Management Department

The Management Department is the minister's department. With his office team, he provides policy planning and analysis for his ministry and coordinates the relationship between the nation and the municipality through exchanges with his deputies in the municipalities. He initiates cooperation with other ministries or citizens in committees and is supported by the Ministry of State Organisation.

The Ministry of Media Affairs, through its media service, provides press and public relations for the ministry, moderates civil dialogue, trains or provides a spokesperson for the minister, writes speeches and texts on request, and ensures the implementation of conferences and events.[14]

The Ministry of Digital Affairs is responsible for digital management and thus provides departmental management. It automatically produces business statistics, staff surveys and the current state of research through statistics. It automatically forwards proposals to the affected or empowered state

11 Ministry of Finance - 8 state revenues, 9 state expenditure
12 Ministry of Labour - 6 Procurement Office
13 Ministry of Digital Affairs - 2.1.2.1.1 Supply of Information Technology
14 Ministry of Media Affairs - 2.2.1.1 Media Service

employees. In document management, it ensures digitalisation and that ministries share forms with each other.[15]

2.3 European Department

The Ministry of Foreign Affairs ensures the constant transmission of the latest information on current European policy affecting the ministry concerned, applicable European Union law and all European Union funding programmes starting or in progress.[16]

2.4 Department for Economy and Enterprises

The Department for Economy and Enterprises drafts laws and ensures compliance with these laws. This includes in particular the requirements vis-à-vis other economic forms, the tax- and Fee-funded benefits of other ministries, and laws on occupational health and safety. It coordinates action with the other ministries and the Minister for Free Market Economy.
The department ensures the implementation of economic and enterprise policy and monitors whether the desired effects are achieved. It negotiates entry fees with the Ministries of Economy and Labour. In the case of many bankruptcies and rising unemployment, it negotiates compensation payments with the Ministry of Planned Economy . In the event of an ongoing industrial dispute, the department can conduct collective bargaining democratically if a majority of affected employers' representatives and labour unions are in favour.

2.5 Department for Economic Sectors of the Free Market Economy

The Department for Economic Sectors of the Free Market Economy coordinates the disposal of surpluses and obsolete or broken assets by the Planned Economy. It may, in voting

---

15 Ministry of Digital Affairs - 2.1.2.1 Digital Service
16 Ministry of Foreign Affairs - 2.4 European Department

with the Ministry of Infrastructure, arrange for the restriction of the real estate market to prevent the large-scale nationwide purchase of land and buildings by Free Market Economy companies. In voting with the ministries of infrastructure, labour and economy, agreements are made on spatial planning. In the finance economy, the department coordinates control over currency, banks and stock exchanges with the ministries of finance and labour. In agriculture, it coordinates the requirements for genetic engineering and medicines with the ministries of labour and health. In foreign trade, it coordinates guest work in voting with the Ministry of Integration and in cooperation with the embassies of the Ministry of Foreign Affairs. It supports labour unions in international labour disputes with the help of the embassies and representations of the Ministry of Foreign Affairs.

2.6 Department for State Services

The Department for State Services coordinates benefit options for companies with the relevant ministries and arranges for tax payments to the Ministries of State Organisation, Media and Family. The other ministries collect their fees directly from the persons or companies.

3 Tasks of the Ministry of Free Market Economy

The task of the ministry for Free Market Economy is to give the companies as much freedom as possible, to impose as few legal requirements as possible and to levy as low taxes as possible. The free market of supply and demand fulfils the steering function. Therefore, enterprise policy is characterised by freedom of contract and provides few legal rights and obligations for employees and companies. The same applies to tenants and landlords, debtors and creditors, consumers and producers. Because in the Free Market Economy workers and production facilities are often relocated between countries, the Ministry of Free Market Economy facilitates international labour disputes and ensures compliance with the requirements on guest work issued by the Ministries of

Labour and Integration.

Economic policy focuses on the economic situation on the world market and requirements from other economic forms. In order to ensure fair competition between companies and to avoid deadweight losses, an entry fee is required for other economic forms.

The Ministry of Free Market Economy pursues a restrained tax policy and accordingly provides only a few Tax-funded services through the Ministries of State Organisation, Media and Family. All other state services are chargeable. Only a few of these fee-based services are required by law, such as audits by the Company Auditing Agency. All other services can be booked voluntarily in order to obtain similar securities as in the Social Market Economy.

4 Economic policy[17]

The Ministry of Free Market Economy operates an economic policy that allows the economic form to exist autonomously. The other economic forms can trade with the Free Market Economy, but have no say in how and with whom work is done. The autonomy of the Free Market Economy can be limited by the constitution and the ministries of labour and health.

The Ministry of Free Market Economy pursues a restrained economic policy that hardly encourages or requires companies. Compared to the other economic forms, the Free Market Economy has the lowest government spending ratio. The state share describes how high the share of state expenditure in the Gross Domestic Product is. Economic freedom is greatest in the Free Market Economy, because mostly only the requirements of the Ministry of Labour apply.

Competition policy does not take place. Fair competition is ensured by the Antitrust Agency.[18] Competition is ensured by the free market, where sufficient demand generates a corresponding supply. Accordingly, there is no structural policy that promotes certain industries and no regional

---

17§210,1,2,4,8 Principles of economic order: BV Art. 94, KV Art.50, §130,2,3 Cultural protection areas and economic zones: BV Art.50
18Ministry of Labour - 15 Antitrust Agency

economic policy that promotes certain regions. Consumer policy is guaranteed by the consumer protection of the Ministry of Labour. The economic policy issues of the labour market and social order are determined by the Ministry of Free Market Economy with the Ministry of Labour. Free Market Economy enterprises are subject to requirements issued by the Ministry of Labour in cooperation with other ministries for all companies and audited by the Company Auditing Agency. To ensure freedom of choice for workers and entrepreneurs between economic forms, the Ministry of Free Market Economy imposes few requirements over other economic forms and no entry fee for switching companies from other economic forms.

4.1 Economic order of the Free Market Economy

The Free Market Economy is managed by the supply and demand of goods or services. Prices are created by the nature and extent of supply and demand. The Ministry of Free Market Economy accepts business start-ups and charges a fee to cover the costs. It ensures economic and contractual freedom and issues necessary exemptions in the interests of the people, the constitution and the environment. The Ministry of Free Market Economy regulates as few companies, goods and services as possible, mainly through the Ministries of Labour and Health.

4.2 Economic development

The Ministry of Free Market Economy monitors global macroeconomic developments and is supported by the embassies and consulates of the Ministry of Foreign Affairs. The aim is to measure the competitiveness of the Free Market Economy's companies on the global market and, if necessary, to improve it. The Ministry of Free Market Economy produces analyses and projections in real laboratories, i.e. in selected or all companies in the Free Market Economy. The key statistics include the growth of turnover and profits, the development of the demographics of the companies' employees, pensioners and applicants. With the help of the key figures, the ministry conducts economic and structural policy research in cooperation with the Company Auditing Agency and the Ministry of Digital Affairs, which provide the necessary data. The goal of the research is a long-term stable increase in prosperity, security and revenues.

5 Switching between economic forms[19]

The freedom of the Free Market Economy is restricted by the other economic forms because they eliminate markets for labour and consumers with whom no trade or only limited trade can be conducted.

The aim of the requirements is to prevent the Free Market Economy from interfering in the markets of other economic forms through international market power. If trade is nevertheless conducted with other economic forms, a legal regularisation must be coordinated with all other ministries of economy and the Ministry of Labour. If a veto quorum of 30% of the affected citizens is met, the negotiation must take place in a committee.[20]

5.1 Entrance and exit of persons and companies

Persons enter the Free Market Economy when they establish a company in the Free Market Economy, enter into an employment contract with a company in the Free Market Economy or purchase products from companies in the Free Market Economy. For companies and persons, entry and exit is possible at any time and there are no entry or exit fees.

Companies can switch to the Free Market Economy at any time if they were founded in another economic form. From the day of the change, the corporate tax rate of the new economic form applies. The Ministry of Finance is responsible for the change of business tax.[21] For the audit of changing companies,

---

19 §186.2 Peaceful separation
20 Ministry of State Organisation - 9.5.14 Veto quorum, 9.6 Committee
21 Ministry of Finance - 5.2.7 Business taxes in the economic forms

the Company Auditing Agency conducts special audits.[22] The laws of the Free Market Economy also apply from the day of the change and are reviewed with the next audit of the Company Auditing Agency. The stricter anti-trust laws ensure free competition in the Free Market Economy and may lead to adjustments in the case of changing companies. Employees must assert their rights themselves against their employer, i.e. the entrepreneur. This is done through negotiations on adjustments in the employment contract and, if necessary, in a collective labour agreement if employees organise themselves in a works council or a labour union.

5.2 Import and export of goods and services

Persons can buy as many goods and services as they want from other states or economic forms as long as they can pay for them. They can also sell their goods and services to persons from other economic forms as long as they can find buyers.

Companies can purchase goods and services from other economic forms for their production as long as they can pay for them. Companies are free to sell goods and services to other economic forms.

However, Free Market Economy companies can only trade with Barter Economy, Planned Economy and Social Market Economy companies or persons that their Ministry of Economy permits.[23] Trade with Social Market Economy companies is only permitted in the national currency, the exchange of which is subject to exchange rate fluctuations.

6 Enterprise policy[24]

The Ministry of Free Market Economy pursues a restrained enterprise policy. It enacts a correspondingly free trade, commercial and handicraft law with few requirements on the principles of corporate governance. The individual sectors can bundle their interests and bring them to the attention of the

22 Ministry of Labour - 10.2.2 Changing companies
23 Ministries of Barter Economy, Planned Economy, Social Market Economy - Import and Export of Goods and Services
24 §228,1,3,4,7 Labour: BV Art. 110, KV Art.39

Ministry of Free Market Economy. The chambers of crafts, industry, trade, advertising, tourism and the liberal professions represent the interests of the sectors.

The ministry ensures a minimum level of protection for employees, consumers and the environment. Employers and employees regulate their own business and professional affairs in treaties. If better conditions are agreed in the treaties than in the laws of the Free Market Economy, this is possible, but worse conditions are not. Individual cases are decided in the Labour Court, which can become precedents and thus create Free Market Economy labour law. The people have a right of co-decision in court decisions through the repeal quorum.

Working conditions are primarily regulated by the employer, secondly by the employers and employees through the employment contract, and thirdly by laws and court decisions.

6.1 Freedom of contract

Every enterprise has the right to conclude treaties with customers or entrepreneurs. Every company has the duty to conclude written employment contracts with all employees. All treaties must be signed by all contracting parties with their real or digital signature and personal data. The contractual partners must be identifiable and give their voluntary consent to the conclusion of the contract. All treaties concluded by companies must be deposited in the labour directory[25] in the digital archive of the Ministry of Free Market Economy within 4 weeks. Treaties deposited there can be viewed by all contracting parties at any time and are notarised.

6.2 Duties for companies[26]

Companies in the Free Market Economy have to fulfil duties imposed on them by the Ministry of Free Market Economy and other ministries by law and by the people through the constitution. These include the following duties. In order

---

25 Ministry of Digital - 12 Directories
26 §190,1,4,8 Environmental protection: KV Art.31, BV Art.74, §234,4 Children's rights, child benefits and parental protection

to adequately inform consumers and achieve near perfect competition, companies must fully inform their customers about the benefits and risks of their products. They have the obligation to label the use of genetically manipulated substances on the goods and services. In order to protect third parties, companies must prevent externalities and price all costs caused by their goods or services into the sales price. To ensure equal employment exchange, companies must report all vacancies in the Labour Directory. In order to protect the environment, companies must only pollute the environment in a regenerative manner so that the pre-pollution state can be restored within one human generation. They have a duty to remedy deficiencies found by the health auditors in voting with the innovation auditors. For parental protection, companies must grant 12 months of unpaid leave to expectant parents after the birth.

6.3 Rights for companies

Setting up a company is free of charge. To open it, a profile must be instituted in the Labour Directory, which automatically opens a People's Bank account at People's Bank[27] for that company. The People's Bank account is free of charge for domestic companies and bears interest at the rate of growth of the Free Market Economy's Gross Domestic Product. Foreigner companies can only use Free Market Economy banks to maintain their business account. If there are other business accounts other than the People's Bank account, an automatic redirection of all account receipts must go through the business tax account at the People's Bank.
Companies have the right to determine the amount of their liability themselves. The purchase and sale of Free Market Economy companies is permitted to all persons and companies and must be regulated in a purchase agreement.

---

27 Ministry of Finance - 11 People's Bank

6.4 Insolvency

Insofar as a company becomes insolvent, all outstanding payments must be made from the proceeds of the sale of the company or its individual parts. First, all taxes, state fees and outstanding wages of the insolvent company's employees must be paid. If the proceeds of the sale are insufficient, the owners are liable with their private assets up to an exemption amount of 10,000 euros. If the company is a joint-stock company, all the entrepreneurs are liable with their private assets up to an exemption amount of 25,000 euros. As soon as the outstanding taxes and wages have been paid, the creditors are served. All creditors have equal rights and receive an equal share of the remaining proceeds from the sale of the company. In addition, the creditors suffer a loss. State payments or state loans to Free Market Economy companies are prohibited, no matter how large the company or corporation.

7 Employee protection

Occupational health and safety standards are lowest in the Free Market Economy. As soon as the weekly working time exceeds 40 hours, 1.5 times the wage must be paid. The wage is determined by the employer in voting with the employee in the employment contract. The 28th day of a month is set for the payment of wages. Leave is unpaid and needs to be authorised by the employer only for family or medical reasons. Insurance for sickness, pension or unemployment is not compulsory.

7.1 Termination

There is no protection against dismissal. Companies are free to choose which employees to dismiss and when. Employees may terminate their employment at any time. A notice period is not prescribed. Employers and workers cooperate voluntarily on both sides. A reason for dismissal is not necessary.

7.2 Collective bargaining

Employees are not required to have a labour union or works council. Wages are specified in the employment contract. Employees must not be restricted in their right to renegotiate their wages and to publish their wage levels on their profile in the Labour Directory at[28] . If there is a labour union, employers may have to form associations and bargain with the union to establish collective labour agreements for all workers in an industry.

7.3 Labour unions

Employees are free to form labour unions. Employers may not prevent them from doing so. Depending on the negotiation between the labour union and the employer or employers' association, the terms of the Social Market Economy may or may not apply. The parties are free to decide what terms are reached through employer and employee representations. Strike and company blockade is a permissible means of industrial action in the Free Market Economy, the form of which is up to the employees. Bodily injury, deprivation of liberty, theft or damage to another's property remain explicit criminal offences, even in industrial action.

The organisation of decision-making in labour unions is basically direct democracy. Membership fees are allowed to finance industrial action and insurance or to buy shares in the industry represented. Labour unions negotiate wages and working conditions with employers and record the agreements in collective labour agreements. If no agreement is reached, a labour union can call for industrial action.

The membership dues of all employees in joint-stock companies are always invested in the purchase of shares in their industry. The more union members there are in a joint-stock company, the more shares in that joint-stock company are bought. The dividends are used to buy even more shares in the industry. Voting shares increase the labour union's influence in management and collective bargaining. If a labour union has

---

28 Ministry of Labour - 13 Labour Directory

a majority of the votes in an industry, the dividends are paid to the members of the union. A committee decides whether each member should receive the same amount per capita or whether it should be distributed according to the total dues paid by a person.

7.3.1 Industrial action

Only labour unions may engage in industrial action. They have the right to call a strike in an industrial dispute. Under the right to strike, workers are allowed to stay away from work with impunity and block state access routes to the company under strike. As soon as at least 10 per cent of the employees of a company are members of a labour union responsible for the occupation, the union is allowed to use the right to strike in that company. A request to block access to a company must be made to the nearest police station. The People's Protection Service blocks public access routes and monitors compliance. Where digital lines are involved, the state supply lines are disconnected. The length of industrial action is at the discretion of the participants. Employers may hire replacement workers, whose employment contracts must be temporary for the duration of a strike.

8 Economic sectors of the Free Market Economy

The economic sectors of the Free Market Economy include the different forms of companies and industries. This allows different rules to be established for different types of enterprises and industry sectors. This is to facilitate cooperation with other economic forms and foreigners.

8.1 Producing companies

Manufacturing companies may produce and sell all products. The products may damage the informed customer, but not third parties. The production of weapons of war is prohibited. Products and production methods that violate the constitution are prohibited. Products must be given a minimum period of time during which the product must function when used properly and as described. A guarantee or refund must be provided within this time frame.

8.2 Service-providing companies

Suppliers are allowed to provide all services. The service of providing security is reserved for state personnel of the Ministry of Security. Services may damage the informed client, but not third parties. Services that violate the constitution are prohibited.

8.3 Private educational institutions[29]

Uniform recognition of educational qualifications must be guaranteed. Private educational institutions coordinate this with the Ministry of Education. To ensure that learners can change educational institutions on an ongoing basis, central performance records are also written in private educational institutions.[30] The examinations are to be taken in the national language, maths, ethics, homeland and subject lessons for primary school and in the national language, maths, a natural science (biology or chemistry or physics), computer science, technology or crafts, ethics and politics. The rating is done by teachers at state educational institutions. Learners have the right to transfer to a state educational institution at any time. Private educational institutions are charged and must pay additional examination fees for their state recognition as part of the Company Auditing Agency[31] to have the curricula and performance of graduates spot-checked. Missions with undercover investigators are also charged in the course of the following audit.

---

29 §177.3 School system: KV Art.43
30 Ministry of Education - 4.6.1 Central performance record
31 Ministry of Labor - 20 Company Auditing Agency

9 Real estate sector[32]

Buyers and sellers of real estate regulate the right of home ownership in the purchase contract. Tenants and landlords have the rights and obligations set out in the tenancy agreement, which both parties conclude voluntarily. This makes them responsible for tenancy law themselves.
Only domestic companies with exclusively domestic owners may be lessors of land inland. The sale of land inland to foreigners is prohibited. Foreign companies or investors may buy or rent buildings, but they may not rent them out.

10 Finance economy

The money market is determined by the European Central Bank, which guards the euro currency. In voting with the Ministry of Foreign Affairs, the Ministry of Free Market Economy can influence decisions of the European Central Bank. The credit and financial market is governed by the rules that investors and debtors have only the contractually agreed rights and obligations. There is a risk of total loss at any time. Foreigners may only invest in companies in the Free Market Economy and agree on voting rights. State liability is excluded, any granting of loans or other state contributions in cash or in kind are prohibited. Insurance companies and policyholders must comply with the contractual benefits they agree with each other.

10.1 Currency[33]

The Free Market Economy trades in the supranational currency, the euro. The supranational currency must be administered by a Central Bank under the authority of all the Finance Ministers of the Member States in an International Union and whose President is directly elected.[34] The Free Market Economy's investments, goods and wages can only be paid in euros.

32§227,1,3 Rental business: BV Art. 109
33§219.3d Central Bank and Currency Policy
34Ministry of Foreign Affairs - 5.8 International Union, 6.4.6 European Union Monetary Union

10.2 Banks[35]

Banks may operate a deposit insurance scheme. No minimum reserve ratio is set. Any state liability or funding to secure a bank against insolvency is prohibited, no matter how large. Insolvent banks will no longer receive loans from the Central Bank. If outstanding repayments to the Central Bank can no longer be made, the bank's customers and owners are liable. If this amount is still not sufficient, the responsible employees are liable with their private assets. If that is not enough either, they must work off the amount due in detention. If the life expectancy is not sufficient for this, all employees of the bank are liable only with their private assets, but must serve a maximum of 10 years in detention. Damage to taxpayers is considered a criminal offence that entails collective guilt of all employees of a bank. In the case of collective detention, the responsible employees are liable first and only if this is not sufficient should it be extended to all employees. In the Free Market Economy, liability through collective guilt is considered an occupational risk.

10.3 Stock exchanges[36]

Free Market Economy companies can operate stock exchanges where shares, bonds and bets can be traded. Entrepreneurs in the Free Market Economy can transform themselves into joint-stock companies and have their shares issued and traded on the exchanges. Whether voting rights or dividends are attached to a share, and if so which, is left to the discretion of the respective company. Foreign countries and companies in the Free Market Economy can issue bonds on the stock exchanges. The issuer determines the amount, maturity and interest rate. Stock exchange companies can issue regulations on which conditions apply to shares, bonds or bets when trading on their stock exchange. To this end, trading partners agree on treaties to which all participants voluntarily commit. Regulations and laws that apply to all exchanges are issued

---

35 §217.1 Banks and insurance companies: BV Art. 98
36 §216,1,5 Joint-stock companies: BV Art. 95, §217,1,2 Banks and insurance companies: BV Art.98

by the Ministry of Labour and reviewed with the Exchange Commission.[37] The VAT rate is levied as tariffs on all dividends and interest payments when they flow abroad.

11 Agriculture[38]

No state subsidies are paid. Groundwater must not be polluted. Toxic substances and genetically modified plants or pesticides must not be released into the environment. All waste must be disposed of in an environmentally neutral manner. The Company Auditing Agency's health auditors check compliance with the standards every two years.

11.1 Genetic engineering

Genetically modified plants must grow in air-filtered greenhouses and greenhouses so that any pollen flight with a risk of fertilisation is excluded. Bees may only be used for pollination if their tribe is exclusively active in the screened greenhouse. The floor of the greenhouse is lined with an impermeable tray containing the plant soil. In case of greenhouse abandonment, this soil must be sterilised to destroy any pollen and seeds.

All products with genetically modified ingredients may be sold. The goods must be clearly labelled as genetically modified for customers. If genetically modified agents were used in the production process, the end product shall be deemed to be genetically modified. No genetically modified products that could be planted or reproduce may be put into circulation. For example, in the case of tomatoes, the seeds could be planted. On the other hand, strained tomatoes or tomato paste are legal.

Genetically modified animals must live in screened enclosures that make escape or entry by other animals impossible. The sale of genetically modified animals is only permitted in a dead state or if it is guaranteed that the animal cannot mate with other genetically unmodified animals or also only lives

---

37 Ministry of Labour - 18.3.3 Exchange Commission
38 §220.1c Agriculture: KV Art.51

under screened conditions.

11.2 Medicine

The use of medical agents that are also used on humans and could lead to resistance of pathogens is prohibited for plants and animals. Better hygiene must be ensured or the death of the animals must be accepted. The further processing of animals that have died as a result of disease into animal feed or fertiliser is only permitted after the germs have been rendered harmless.

12 Foreign trade[39]

The Ministry of Free Market Economy regulates European and international economic issues in voting with the Ministry of Foreign Affairs. Foreign trade in goods, services and companies are regulated in trade contracts. The contracting parties are involved in the contract negotiations. All trade contracts concluded are published in the Labour Directory and must not contradict the constitution. The people have a right of co-decision through the repeal quorum.[40] The Ministry of Free Market Economy votes on international economic and monetary issues jointly with the Ministries of Foreign Affairs and Labour and the people.

12.1 International industrial action

Employees of companies with locations in different countries can join together in international industrial action through their labour unions. Labour unions can use their membership fees in solidarity to reimburse lost wages during strikes in all countries. If there is no labour union in a country, domestic unions, in voting with the Ministry of Foreign Affairs and embassies, can provide training to foreign citizens working in the affected companies on how to form a union.

---

39 §225,1,7 Foreign trade policy: BV Art. 101
40 Ministry of State Organisation - 9.5.15 Repeal quorum

12.2 Guest work

Companies are allowed to hire guest workers from abroad as long as the requirements for wages, employment contracts, quota of foreigners, immigration procedures and family reunification are met.[41]

12.2.1 Wage

The companies support their guest workers with board, lodging and medical care. The first living space inland is rented by the companies. The guest workers have the right to look for other accommodation at any time and to pay for it themselves. The wage must be sufficient to finance the health insurance contribution, local rent and living expenses.

12.2.2 Employment contracts

The duration of employment contracts with guest workers must be limited to a maximum of 3 years. Permanent employment contracts may only be concluded if the guest worker has been successfully naturalised[42] and the wage is sufficient for the child support of his or her family. Permanent employment contracts may be terminated by the Ministry of Free Market Economy if the following conditions are met. Termination without notice if the guest worker or a family member commits a criminal offence inland. Termination occurs if the guest worker or a family member becomes indebted inland and thus in need of social assistance. The awarding of permanent contracts, the extension of existing fixed-term contracts and the conclusion of new employment contracts with guest workers is no longer permitted once the quota of foreigners is exceeded.
If the employment contract is terminated and another employment contract is not concluded within 3 months, the labour migration visa ends and there is an immediate

---

41 Ministry of Integration - 7.5.2 Guest work, 7.4 Quota of foreigners, 7.5 Immigration conditions
42 Ministry of Integration - 4.2.3 Naturalised foreigners

obligation to leave the country. Delays are punishable by law.[43]

12.2.3 Quota of foreigners

If the municipal quota of foreigners is reached, guest workers are not allowed to live or work there. If the national quota of foreigners is exceeded, no new employment contracts may be concluded with guest workers. Temporary treaties expire. If the quota of foreigners still does not fall below the limit, they are deported. A survey is launched among remaining guest workers to find out who would like to emigrate again. Voluntary foreigners are allowed to terminate their employment contracts without notice.

A survey is also carried out among companies with guest workers to find out who can replace guest workers with permanent contracts with domestic workers. Voluntary companies are then allowed to terminate open-ended employment contracts with guest workers without notice.

If there are not enough voluntary foreigners, single and childless guest workers are first selected by lot and deported. The Ministry of Integration takes care of the procedure.[44]

12.2.4 Immigration procedures for guest workers

Companies must apply for a labour migration visa for their application and recruitment process with guest workers on the ministry's Free Market Economy intranet site.

The Ministry of Free Market Economy approves the application if the quota of foreigners is not exceeded and the guest worker is crime-free and debt-free. Corresponding evidence must be collected and submitted by the company during the application process.

The Ministry of Free Market Economy sends the approved application to the Ministry of Foreign Affairs. At the embassy of the guest worker's country, the information is checked again. The guest worker must complete the application for

---

43 Ministry of Justice - 8.18.1 Visa overstay for guest workers
44 Ministry of Integration - 7.9 Exit procedures

a work migration visa with his signature at the embassy in his country of origin and receives a blue identity card with the word "guest worker" on it. This identity card contains a photograph, name, place and date of birth and the period for which the labour migration visa is valid. The identity card entitles him or her to entry and temporary residence inland. The guest worker must always carry this identity card with him/her inland. Foreigners with unlimited residence permits only have the identity card for naturalised persons.

12.2.5 Family reunion

If the employment contract is extended indefinitely, the wage is sufficient to support a family and the guest worker has been successfully naturalised, the family may join them. The foreigner family must then inform the Ministry of Integration within 12 months whether the inland is to become their new homeland or whether they want to return to their country of origin in the future. Family members seeking a permanent residence permit inland must become naturalised persons. Otherwise, the family must emigrate when all children are of age of majority.

13 Tax policy[45]

Business tax of 20% is levied on all incoming remittances and deposits to the business account through the People's Bank Tax Account. Turnover is taxed. Losses cannot be claimed. If taxes cannot be paid, the company is insolvent. Insolvency proceedings follow. For the purpose of economic policy coordination, the ministry can adjust the corporate tax rates to industries or company sizes.

Customers have to pay value added tax on services provided by the companies. Customers of financial services are charged 20% value added tax on their investment income directly from the financial company to the Ministry of Finance. If the investment income flows abroad, 20% tariffs is levied.

45§150,1,3d,4 Business taxes

13.1 Financial policy

The Ministry of Free Market Economy uses the revenues from business taxes to fund its expenditure, which is not Fee-funded. Business taxes are adjusted to the amount necessary to finance Tax-funded benefits to companies and compensation payments to Planned Economy.

13.2 State orders

Public orders may only be awarded to Free Market Economy companies if there are no companies in the Social Market Economy and Planned Economy that can do the orders. The Procurement Review Board must approve state orders to Free Market Economy companies.[46]

14 State services

State services are available in the Free Market Economy, but mostly for a fee. The other economic forms decide which state services they offer as insurance, subscription or individual service. Any state service to foreigners may only be fulfilled if there are no more domestic nationals in need.

14.1 Tax-funded state services

In the Free Market Economy, governance is left to the companies. If companies or industry associations decide to run their company democratically with the participation of all employees, they will receive free support from the ministries of media and digital.

State services that are not chargeable but Tax-funded even for companies in the Free Market Economy are the following services provided by the Ministries of State Organisation, Media, Family and Foreign Affairs.

46Ministry of Labour - 20.7.1.3 Procurement Review Board

14.1.1 Ministry of State Organisation

The Ministry of State Organisation ensures a functioning state apparatus that guarantees legal certainty for the companies in their ventures.

14.1.2 Ministry of Media Affairs

The Ministry of Media Affairs ensures that information on economic and state processes functions properly in order to guarantee lawful procedures for the companies.

14.1.3 Ministry of Family Affairs

The Ministry of Family Affairs provides a caring civil society in which companies keep their workforce healthy and motivated. For children, it pays the child benefit[47] with which they have the same opportunities as all children, regardless of the economic form.

14.2 Fee-funded state services

The following services provided by the state are Fee-funded and voluntary, unless otherwise provided by the affected ministry. The amount of the fees is determined by the ministry responsible. If no other determination is specified, the fee shall be equal to the coverage of all expenses plus a 10% profit mark-up.

14.2.1 Ministry of Labour

14.2.1.1 Unemployment agency

Employment exchange services provided by the Ministry of Labour through the Labour Directory are free of charge. Other employment exchange services for jobs in Free Market Economy companies are chargeable. The Ministry of Labour

47Ministry of Family Affairs - 8.4 Child benefit

determines the amount of the costs.

14.2.1.2 Company audit

The companies must be audited by the Company Auditing Agency every 2 years for a fee. The audits to determine whether the companies pay sufficient taxes, meet environmental protection standards and do not commit any criminal offences[48] are mandatory. The audits of whether the companies provide sufficient occupational safety and health, are economically viable, provide safe goods and services or are innovative can be booked as an individual service up to 4 weeks before the audit. Economic auditors perform the necessary audits for the Antitrust Agency and the Exchange Commission. Management consultancy can be booked upon motions. The costs for the audits and advice are determined by the Company Auditing Agency.

14.2.2 Ministry of Foreign Affairs

The Ministry of Foreign Affairs ensures that all other countries are assessed to determine the level of tariffs or admissibility of guest workers. The Ministry of Foreign Affairs issues licences for the import and export of capital, goods and services in voting with the Ministry of Free Market Economy. All commercial contracts entered into by companies in the Free Market Economy must be available at all times to the Ministries of Foreign Affairs and Free Market Economy through the Labour Directory. The Ministry of Foreign Affairs charges fees for its services to all companies involved.

---

48 Ministry of Labor - 20 Company Auditing Agency

14.2.3 Ministry of Planned Economy

14.2.3.1 Compensation payments[49]

The Ministry of Planned Economy obliges the Ministry of Free Market Economy to make compensatory payments to unemployed and impoverished pensioners who have derived at least 60% of their income from the Free Market Economy in their previous working life. Free Market Economy companies have to pay higher business taxes for compensation payments.

14.2.4 Ministry of Social Market Economy

14.2.4.1 Unemployment

The Ministry of Social Market Economy offers unemployment insurance. The unemployed then receive 80% of their last salary for 12 months from the date of unemployment.[50]

14.2.4.2 Pension[51]

The Ministry of Social Market Economy offers the state pension insurance and automatically links it to Citizens' Insurance[52] . Companies can make pension contributions for their employees, but they do not have to. Employees can also book the state pension insurance as private provision. Companies are not allowed to force employees into early retirement in order to make redundancies at the expense of the pension insurance.

49§45.4 Welfare state
50Ministry of Social Market Economy - 17.5.3 Unemployment Insurance
51§232,1,2b,2c Occupational benefits: BV Art. 113
52Ministry of Social Market Economy - 17.5.4 Pension Insurance, Ministry of Labour - 10.2.4 Citizens' Insurance

14.2.5 Ministry of Education[53]

All educational programmes up to the college entrance qualification are Tax-funded, mostly through child benefits. All subsequent vocational education and training is Fee-funded. State institutions of the Ministry of Education can be attended for the training of professionals and the qualification of volunteers. Digital education via the Knowledge Directory is free of charge; subsequent final examinations are subject to a fee. Fees are only payable if persons complete their educational qualification and then take up or continue employment in a Free Market Economy company.

The costs are calculated from the sum of the value of the premises and the institution used per hour, the hourly wage of the teaching and service staff, divided by the number of participants in the lessons or examination.

14.2.5.1 Vocational training[54]

Professional trainings are subject to fees for entrepreneurs and Free Market Economy employees. Payments are made per head until 110% of the training costs of a skilled worker are covered. The deciding factor is whether the educational qualifications were taken at a state or private educational institution. Fees are only payable for state educational qualifications. The Company Auditing Agency checks the CVs of entrepreneurs and employees via the Education Directory and collects the costs as part of the audit. Reserves must be set aside for each employee on a monthly basis, equivalent to a set amount. The reserves are collected by the tax auditors at the time of the audit by the Company Auditing Agency and remitted to the Ministry of Education. The amount is set by the Ministry of Education in voting with the Ministry of Labour. It is equal to the cost of an educational qualification and is lower if tuition was replaced by self-study via the Knowledge Directory and only the final examination incurred costs. It does not apply if companies train the skilled worker themselves on the job.

---

53 §177,1 School system: BV Art. 62, §178.2 Education contributions
54 §181.3 Vocational training

In this case, the educational programme is offered as a fixed price and is deducted in equal monthly parts from the profits for the entrepreneur or from the salary for the employee. Entrepreneurs can rate the training content of the training pathways for their workers in the Company Auditing Agency's questionnaires. Depending on how well individual contents are rated, the Ministry of Education can adjust the curriculum accordingly.

14.2.5.2 Vocational further training[55]

Professional training has a fixed price, which makes it possible for companies in the Free Market Economy to book training units in the state educational institutions for entrepreneurs or employees. The fees must be paid at the beginning of the training and are set by the Ministry of Education.

14.2.6 Ministry of Finance

The Ministry of Finance determines for which countries or goods tariffs are to be set for exports and imports and how high they are to be. It makes enquiries with the embassies. The fees for these services are charged to the companies together with the tariffs.

14.2.7 Ministry of Health

Private or state health insurance companies are liable to pay costs. Companies can provide health insurance for their employees in whole or in part, but they do not have to. Physicians may provide all services with their own set prices. The Ministry of Health sets standards for the examination of physicians, which are reviewed by health auditors as part of the final examinations of a medical education programme and audits of practices. The costs of the health auditors and development of the standards are included in the examination fees.

55§182.1 Further education: BV Art. 64a

14.2.8 Ministry of Infrastructure

Companies must pay for connection to the networks of road, rail, data, electricity and water, as well as pay an annual fee for the use of state networks. The price is based on cost recovery plus 10% profit. A fee must be paid for data, electricity and water, both for private and state suppliers. Selling or renting a property through the Real Estate Directory costs 0.2% of the sale proceeds or rent before tax deduction.

14.2.9 Ministry of Innovation

Companies must pay a levy to start a research project in Innovation Labs and state educational institutions or other funding from the Ministry of Innovation, which is based on and covers 110% of the expenditure. Innovation auditors must be appointed for a fee 4 weeks before the Company Auditing Agency audit in order to use the services.

14.2.10 Ministry of Integration

The Ministry of Integration invoices each company for the integration services as a monthly amount for each guest worker hired, including all their family members who have joined them.

14.2.11 Ministry of Digital Affairs

Foreigner companies are not allowed to use the intranet. Domestic citizens must make a regular contribution if they use the intranet as a distribution channel or for digital administration. The creation of a website for the company with all necessary sales mechanisms is charged as a single service. This allows the sales function to be downloaded from the Labour Directory as an internet version and synchronised on an ongoing basis.

14.2.12 Ministry of Justice

Court personnel and legal representations in court proceedings in which the companies are involved are subject to a fee. Joining the state legal expenses insurance is possible, but not obligatory.[56] If companies wish to use prisoners for cooperation, the number to be paid is determined by the Ministry of Justice.

14.2.13 Ministry of Security

Security companies are prohibited. Security services shall only be provided by the Ministry of Security. All persons, animals or machines that provide security through the use of physical force must be able to be democratically controlled. They are sworn to serve the will of the people.
Security services for companies are provided at a charge by the People's Protection Service.[57] Prices are based on cost recovery plus 10% profit. Deployments of security forces to maintain public order, which become necessary due to activities of the clients or the company, will be charged to the company. The amount of the charge depends on the quantity and duration of the personnel deployed. For example, police operations during football matches have to be paid by the football clubs or the extinguishing of a fire on the company's premises or by products of the company.

15 Switching to the new system

The template for the Free Market Economy is the US economy.[58] In the transition, the economic form in the country consists of a mixed form between a free and a social market economy. The first task of this ministry is to separate the two economic forms and create separate areas of accountability.

56Ministry of Justice - 5.7.7 Legal expenses insurance
57Ministry of Security - 6 People's Protection Service
58https://de.usembassy.gov/de/arbeitsrecht/ Status: February 2000

15.1 Conversion of the old ministries

The following is a list of all the departments and units that are transferring to the Ministry of Free Market Economy. If only the department or sub-department is named, all its units are transferred. If individual units are named, only those units are transferred. All departments and units not named are dropped. Existing staff adapt their tasks to the new requirements. The corresponding names of the units can usually be found as keywords in the running text.

15.1.1 Federal Ministry for Economic Affairs and Energy[59]

I Economic policy
Fundamental issues of economic policy, economic policy issues of the labour market and social order, fiscal policy, economic policy coordination, tax policy
Competition and structural policy, consumer policy, fundamental competition policy issues of digitalisation, regional economic policy, money, credit and financial markets, real estate sector
Macroeconomic development, analyses and projections, economic policy analysis, real laboratories, observation, analysis and projection of macroeconomic development, growth, demography, statistics, economic and structural policy research

VII SME policy
Service industry, trade and advertising industry, tourism policy
Crafts, Chambers of Commerce and Industry, Promotion of Crafts and Trades, Liberal Professions, Trade Law

15.1.2 Federal Ministry of Justice and Consumer Protection[60]

III Trade and Commercial Law
Corporate constitution

59https://www.bmwi.de/Redaktion/DE/Downloads/M-O/
organisationsplan-bmwi.pdf?__blob=publicationFile Version: 15.02.2019
60https://www.bmjv.de/SharedDocs/Downloads/DE/Ministerium/
Organisationsplan/Organisationsplan_DE.pdf;jsessionid=A807B5B1F5E
FC74825E8B2A6508405BE.2_cid297?__blob=publicationFile&v=131
Viewed on: 14/05/2019

Foreign trade law, trade and craft law, insurance law, fee law in the field of industrial property protection

15.1.3 Bavarian State Ministry of Justice[61]

D Civil law and consumer law
Tenancy law and condominium law

---

61 https://www.justiz.bayern.de/media/pdf/orgplan/
organigramm__18042019.pdf Status: 18.04.2019

Contact form

Dear reader
If you would like to make what you have read come true, in
whole or in part, together with other like-minded people, I
offer you several possibilities with this contact form. Fill it
out, tear out the page and send it by post to:
Andreas Seidl, P.O. Box 1206, 63488 Seligenstadt / Germany

Or send the details to:
Phone: 0049 1522 818 2243 (whatsapp, telegram, signal)
Email: andreas.seidl2022@web.de

Please mark with a cross:
O   I want to found a dynamic People's Party.
O   I want to donate money for implementation.
O   I want contacts with like-minded people in my area.

Forename: ______________________________________

Surname: ______________________________________

Please fill in only the contact option through which a reply
should be made.

Street, house no.:   ____________________________________

Postcode, city, country: ____________________________________

Phone: ____________________________________

Email address: ____________________________________